3. Look at the examples and think about
when you wou...

D0629194

Irregular verbs

Most verbs in the past tense end in the
letters **ed**.

However, some verbs do not follow this
pattern and they are called **irregular verbs**.
Here are some irregular verbs:

Present tense	Past tense
I am	I was
I catch	I caught
I eat	I ate
I get	I got
I make	I made
I run	I ran
I see	I saw
I swim	I swam

21

---

4. Try making up new examples of your own.

Written by Emily Guille-Marrett
Illustrated by Ian Cunliffe

Published by Ladybird Books Ltd
A Penguin Company
Penguin Books Ltd, 80 Strand, London WC2R 0RL, UK
Penguin Books Australia Ltd, Camberwell, Victoria, Australia
Penguin Books (NZ) Ltd, Cnr Airbourne and Rosedale Roads, Albany, Auckland, 1310, New Zealand

3 5 7 9 10 8 6 4

© LADYBIRD BOOKS MMIV

Printed in Italy

Grammar
and
Punctuation
for School

Nouns

Common nouns are the names given to general things or people.

tree

chair

mouse

ball

man

woman

A noun is a word used to name things.

Proper nouns are the names given to people, places and official titles. Proper nouns always start with a capital letter.

Ben   Anjani   Marco   Rachel

Jamaica

New York

Queen Victoria

President Chirac

7

Nouns – continued

Collective nouns are the names given to groups of things.

team

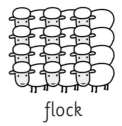

flock

litter

herd

swarm

bouquet

A noun is a word used to name things.

Abstract nouns are the names given to feelings or thoughts.

anger

love

hope

courage

joy

wisdom

Singular and plural

Plurals usually end in the letter **s** but some do not and we call these irregular.

Singular (one thing)   **Plural** (two or more)

cat | cats

book | books

car | cars

skirt | skirts

dish | dishes

baby | babies

child | children

knife | knives

Singular means just one thing.
Plural means more than one thing.

Some nouns have just one word for both singular and plural. They cannot be counted like ordinary nouns.

butter

sand

water

money

flour

snow

Pronouns

Here are two ways of writing the same thing.

1. Millie likes to dance. **Millie** dances every day.

2. Millie likes to dance. **She** dances every day.

The second example uses the personal pronoun **she** to avoid repeating the proper noun **Millie**. This makes the sentences read in a smoother way.

A pronoun is often used to take the place of a noun in a sentence to avoid repeating it.

There are a number of different ways to use a **pronoun**.

1. Here are some examples of **personal pronouns** replacing nouns.

He plays rugby.

They like eating oranges.

The baby rattled **it**.

Grandma made **us** a cake.

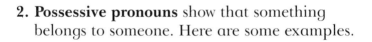

2. **Possessive pronouns** show that something belongs to someone. Here are some examples.

The computer is **mine**.

The games are **yours**.

The toys are **ours**.

The book is **his** not **hers**.

Adjectives

Adjectives have been used to describe the noun **dog** in the pictures below.

big dog

small dog

white dog

brown dog

muddy dog

spotty dog

An adjective gives us information about a noun or a pronoun.

thin dog

fat dog

fast dog

wet dog

hairy dog

greedy dog

Adjectives can be used to compare two or more things or people.

small   smaller   smallest

fast   faster   fastest

muddy   muddier   muddiest

An adjective gives us information about a noun or a pronoun.

Using adjectives can make your writing more interesting. Try using different adjectives when you write.

big
colossal, enormous, gigantic, huge, large, massive, mighty

cross
angry, annoyed, frustrated, fuming, irate, miffed

happy
content, delighted, ecstatic, enchanted, merry, overjoyed

pretty
beautiful, handsome, lovely, picturesque radiant, stunning

If you find yourself using the same word and you can't think of something else, use a book called a **thesaurus** to help you find different words.

Verbs tell us the different actions the children make in the pictures below.

walk

run

eat

drink

play

ride

A verb tells us what is happening in a sentence. It is a 'doing' word.

jump

hop

wait

read

swim

sleep

Verb tenses

Verbs can tell us when something happens.

1. Verbs in the present tense tell us that
something is happening now.

I paint a picture.

I am painting a picture.

2. Verbs in the past tense tell us that
something has taken place.

I painted a picture.

I was painting a picture.

3. Verbs in the future tell us that something
is going to happen. The word **will** is often
used to show the future.

I will paint a picture tomorrow.

Irregular verbs

Most verbs in the past tense end in the
letters **ed**.

However, some verbs do not follow this
pattern and they are called **irregular verbs**.
Here are some irregular verbs:

Present tense	Past tense
I am	I was
I catch	I caught
I eat	I ate
I get	I got
I make	I made
I run	I ran
I see	I saw
I swim	I swam

Adverbs

1. Some **adverbs** tell us **how** something happens. They usually end in the letters **ly**.

He ran home **quickly**.

I shouted **loudly**.

She played the piano **beautifully**.

An adverb adds to the meaning of a verb or gives the sentence additional information.

2. Some **adverbs** tell us **when** something happens.

I have a ballet class **now**.

The bus will be here **soon**.

We have maths **after** break.

Adverbs – continued

3. Some **adverbs** tell us **where** something happens.

It was too wet to play **outside**.

The rabbit hopped **away**.

I ran **home**.

An adverb adds to the meaning of a verb or gives the sentence additional information.

4. Some **adverbs** tell us by **how much** something happens.

The tortoise is **really** slow.

We **almost** missed the train.

It was **too** cold to eat ice cream.

5. Some adverbs tell us **how often** something happens.

I brush my teeth **regularly**.

My friend **never** lies.

We **always** eat fruit.

Sentences

A written **sentence** always starts with a capital letter and usually ends with a **full stop (.)**.

Charlie opened his birthday presents.

↓   ↓

capital letter   full stop

A sentence ends in a full stop, question mark or an exclamation mark.

If a question is being asked, a sentence ends with a **question mark (?)**.

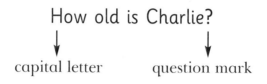

How old is Charlie?

↓ capital letter   ↓ question mark

To express emotion, like surprise, some written sentences end with an **exclamation mark (!)**.

The party was a big surprise!

↓ capital letter   ↓ exclamation mark

Commas

A **comma (,)** is used to help sentences make more sense by breaking them up into smaller portions.

Although it was sunny, it felt cold outside.

Here are two more examples of how a comma can be used.

1. To separate items in a list.

I like to eat fish, rice, peas and beans.

2. To add extra information within a sentence.

Jane, my sister, is only two years old.

Speech marks

We use **speech marks** (" ") to show that someone is speaking. All the spoken words must go inside the speech marks.

A comma is used to separate the spoken words from the unspoken words.

"The glass slipper is mine," said Cinderella.
"It won't fit," said the ugly sisters.

A comma is not needed if the sentence ends in a question mark or an exclamation mark.

"Will you marry me?" asked the Prince.
"Yes!" Cinderella replied.

Apostrophes

1. The apostrophe can be used to show a missing letter or letters when words are shortened.

It's snowing. Let's make a snowman!

I have	I've
I am	I'm
it is	it's
I will	I'll
they have	they've
we are	we're
did not	didn't
could not	couldn't